# Plants

# Leaves

## Patricia Whitehouse

Heinemann Library
Chicago, Illinois

Customer Service  888-454-2279
Visit our website at www.heinemannlibrary.com

Designed by Sue Emerson/Heinemann Library, Page layout by Carolee A. Biddle
Printed and bound in the U.S.A. by Lake Book

06 05 04 03 02
10 9 8 7 6 5 4 3 2 1

**Library of Congress Cataloging-in-Publication Data**
Whitehouse, Patricia, 1958-
   Leaves / Patricia Whitehouse.
      p. cm. — (Plants)
Includes index.
Summary: A basic introduction to leaves, describing their physical
characteristics, function, and uses.
   ISBN 1-58810-521-0 (HC), 1-58810-730-2 (Pbk.)
   1. Leaves—Juvenile literature. [1. Leaves.] I. Title. II. Plants
(Des Plaines, Ill.)
   QK649 .W45 2002
   581.4'8—dc21

                              2001003650

**Acknowledgments**
The author and publishers are grateful to the following for permission to reproduce copyright material:
Title page, pp. 8, 15, 23d Dwight Kuhn; pp. 4, 9, 21, 22, 23a, 23b, 24 E. R. Degginger/Color Pic, Inc.; pp. 5, 23e Gary W. Carter/Visuals Unlimited; p. 6 Lynn M. Stone; p. 7 Gerald Van Dyke/Visuals Unlimited; p. 10 Jack Glisson; p. 11 Chris Steele/Perkins/Magnum/PictureQuest; p. 12 Richard Shiell; p. 13 Joseph Kayne/Willard Clay Photography, Inc.; p. 14 Wally Eberhart/Visuals Unlimited; pp. 16, 18 Amor Montes de Oca; p. 17 Willard Clay Photography, Inc.; p. 19, 23c Eileen R. Herrling; p. 20 Peter Gregg/Color Pic, Inc.

Cover photograph courtesy of Amor Montes de Oca

Every effort has been made to contact copyright holders of any material reproduced in this book.
Any omissions will be rectified in subsequent printings if notice is given to the publisher.

Special thanks to our advisory panel for their help in the preparation of this book:

Eileen Day, Preschool Teacher
Chicago, IL

Paula Fischer, K–1 Teacher
Indianapolis, IN

Sandra Gilbert,
Library Media Specialist
Houston, TX

Angela Leeper,
Educational Consultant
North Carolina Department
of Public Instruction
Raleigh, NC

Pam McDonald, Reading Teacher
Winter Springs, FL

Melinda Murphy,
Library Media Specialist
Houston, TX

Helen Rosenberg, MLS
Chicago, IL

Anna Marie Varakin,
Reading Instructor
Western Maryland College

The publishers would also like to thank Anita Portugal, a master gardener at the Chicago Botanic Garden, for her help in reviewing the contents of this book for accuracy.

Some words are shown in bold, **like this.**
You can find them in the picture glossary on page 23.

# Contents

# What Are Leaves?

branch

Leaves are a part of any plant.

They grow on the **branches** of trees.

4

stem

vine

Leaves grow on other plants, too.

Leaves grow on these grape **stems** and **vines.**

# Why Do Plants Have Leaves?

Leaves make food for plants.

They use water, air, and sunlight to make the food.

Leaves help plants breathe.

Holes in the leaves let air in and out.

# Where Do Leaves Come From?

seed

leaf

Leaves begin inside seeds.

You can see a tiny leaf inside this seed.

When a plant is grown, new leaves grow inside the **buds.**

Then, the leaves pop out of the buds.

# How Big Are Leaves?

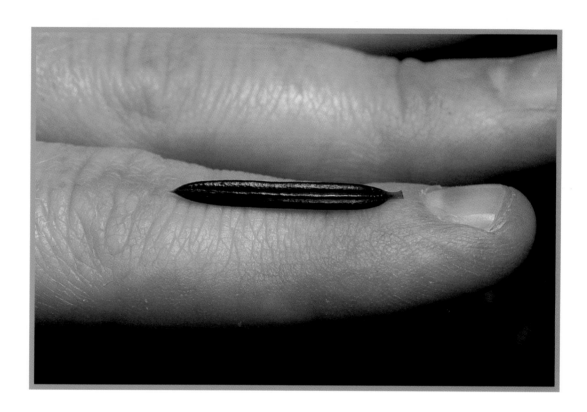

Leaves come in many sizes.

Some leaves can fit on your finger.

Some leaves are as big as
your hand.

Some leaves are almost as big
as you are!

# How Many Leaves Can Plants Have?

Some plants have just a few leaves.

This desert lily has a few leaves.

Some plants have hundreds
of leaves.

Look at all the leaves on this
maple tree.

# What Shapes Are Leaves?

Leaves have lots of different shapes.

They can be thin or round or have pointy edges.

But leaves on one plant are all
the same shape.

# What Colors Are Leaves?

Most leaves are green.

But leaves can be red or purple or have stripes or dots.

In some places, leaves turn colors in the fall.

Then, the leaves can be red or gold.

# How Do People Use Leaves?

People use leaves for food.

When you eat lettuce, you are eating leaves.

roof

People use leaves to make things.

This **roof** is made of leaves.

# How Do Animals Use Leaves?

Animals use leaves for food.

This rabbit is eating leaves.

Animals use leaves to build their homes.

This squirrel nest is made of leaves.

# Quiz

Do you remember what leaves do for plants?

Look for the answers on page 24.

# Picture Glossary

**bud**
page 9

**stem**
page 5

**branch**
page 4

**vine**
page 5

**roof**
page 19

# Note to Parents and Teachers

Reading for information is an important part of a child's literacy development. Learning begins with a question about something. Help children think of themselves as investigators and researchers by encouraging their questions about the world around them. Each chapter in this book begins with a question. Read the question together. Look at the pictures. Talk about what you think the answer might be. Then read the text to find out if your predictions were correct. Think of other questions you could ask about the topic, and discuss where you might find the answers. Assist children in using the picture glossary and the index to practice new vocabulary and research skills.

# Index

**Answers to quiz on page 22**

Leaves make food for plants.

Leaves help plants breathe.